CHOCOLATE

Favourite Foods

Cake
Chips
Chocolate
Ice-Cream
Milkshake
Pizza

All words that appear in **bold** are explained in the glossary on page 30

First published in 1992 by
Wayland (Publishers) Ltd
61 Western Road, Hove
East Sussex BN3 1JD, England
© Copyright 1992 Wayland (Publishers) Ltd

Editor: Francesca Motisi
Research: Anne Moses and Mike and Maria Gordon

British Library Cataloguing in Publication Data
Moses, Brian
    Chocolate.—(Favourite Foods Series)
    I. Title   II. Gordon, Mike   III. Series
    641.2

    ISBN 0-7502-0607-1

Typeset by Dorchester Typesetting Group Ltd
Printed and bound in Belgium by Casterman, S.A.

CHOCOLATE

Written by Brian Moses

Illustrated by Mike Gordon

Wayland

Chocolate is fun to eat at any time –

decorations from the
tree at Christmas,

a bar of chocolate
at the cinema,

Easter Eggs filled
with chocolate
buttons,

or sneaking the soft
centres from Mum's
birthday present!

The Aztecs of Mexico enjoyed drinking chocolate over five hundred years ago. They called their drink *Chocolatl.*

A Spanish **explorer** called Cortes took the recipe back to Spain.

Soon rich people in Europe began
drinking chocolate in Chocolate Houses.

COCOA ALWAYS READY

These were like cafés, where you could
enjoy a cup of chocolate.

Later on in history, people began to eat chocolate instead of just drinking it.

A factory in Switzerland produced the first factory-made block of chocolate in 1819.

Chocolate became cheaper and everyone could buy and enjoy it.

Chocolate is made from cocoa.
Cocoa is made from the beans that grow
in pods on cocoa trees.

Cocoa trees grow mostly in Africa
and in the **tropical rainforests** of
South America.

In each cocoa pod there are between twenty and forty beans.

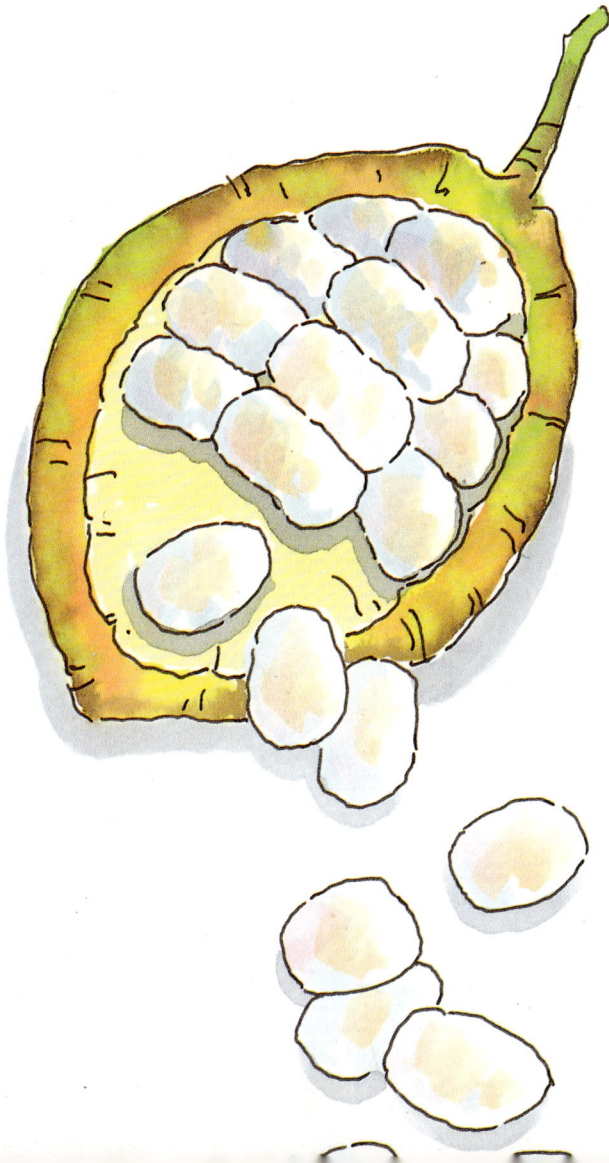

These beans are packed inside a heap of banana leaves for several days, while a change takes place called **fermentation**.

The heat inside the heap brings out the chocolate flavour.

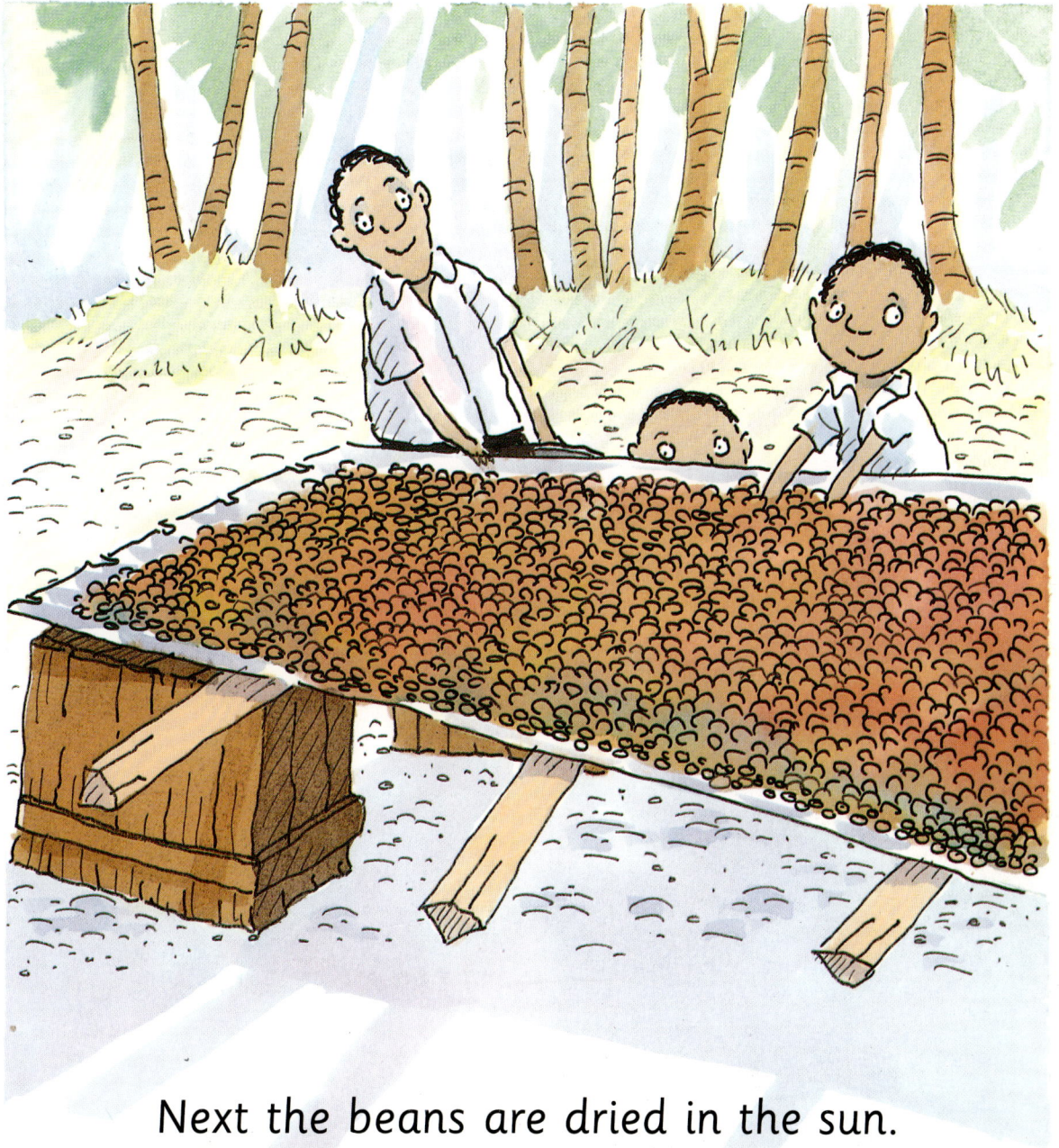

Next the beans are dried in the sun.

After drying the
cocoa beans are
shipped to other
countries.

Then they are
unloaded and
taken to factories
by truck.

At the factories the beans are . . .

cleaned,

sorted . . .

LIGHT

MEDIUM

DARK

and roasted.

cocoa beans

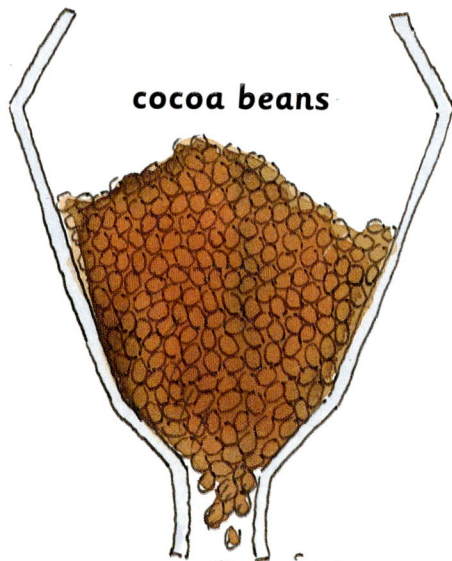

Next the shells of the beans are blown away by jets of air. This leaves the middle of the bean which is called the nib.

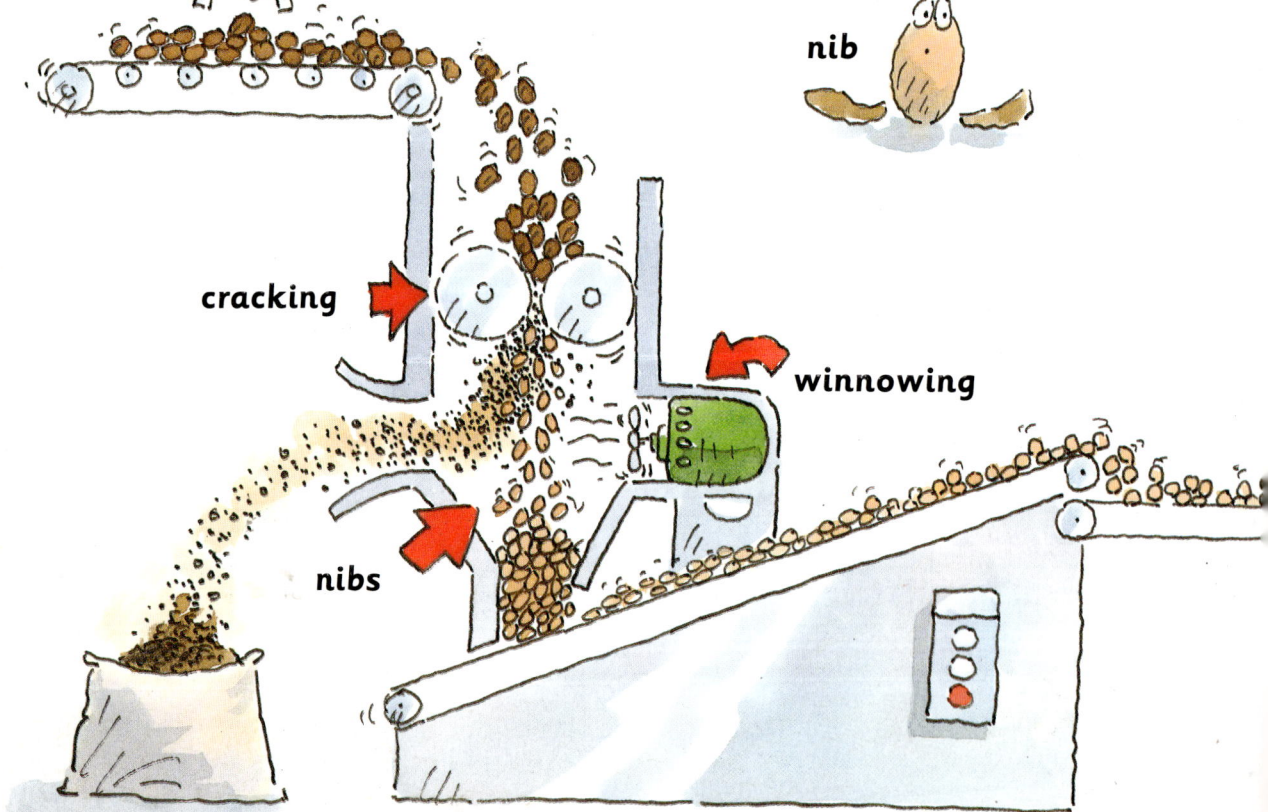

nib

cracking

winnowing

nibs

The nibs are then taken
on a moving belt towards
steel rollers. Here they
are ground into
a thick liquid
called **cocoa mass**.

grinding nibs

cocoa mass

The cocoa mass is then pressed until all the fat is squeezed out. This is called **cocoa butter**. Chocolate powder is left behind.

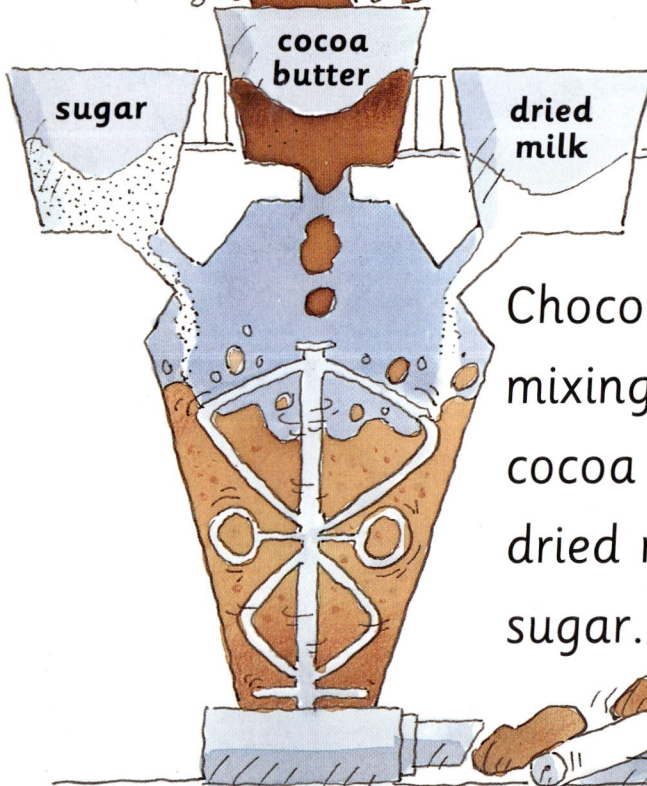

sugar

cocoa butter

dried milk

Chocolate is made by mixing cocoa mass and cocoa butter with dried milk and sugar.

To make sure the chocolate doesn't taste gritty the mixture is then crushed between large rollers.

The mixture is now stirred and beaten for many hours in a huge machine called a **conche**. This makes the chocolate really smooth and also adds air and water to the recipe.

The chocolate is kept hot so that it doesn't set. It is poured into moulds, or sprayed round soft centres in special machines.

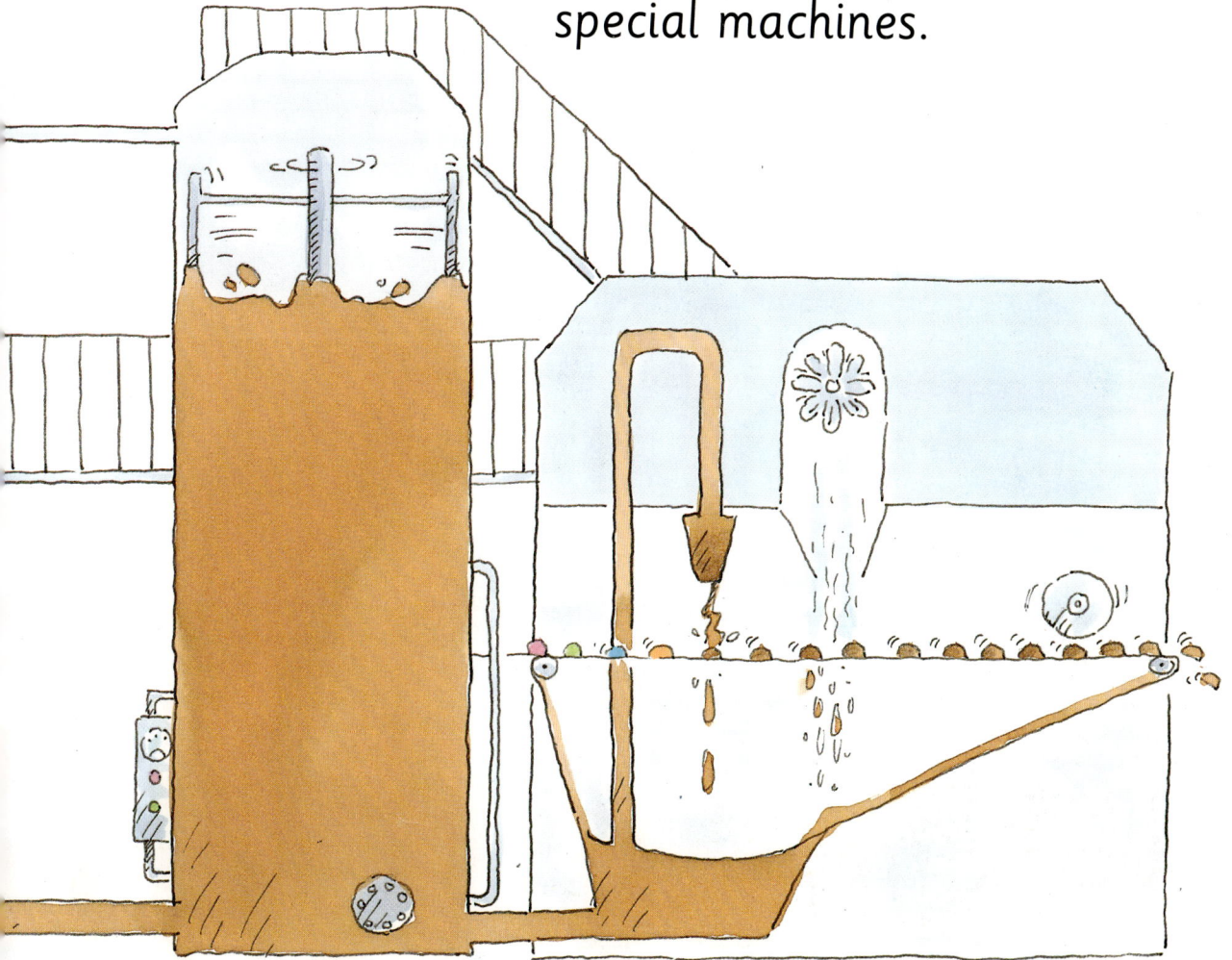

Different kinds of chocolate are made by mixing in nuts, sultanas and raisins. How many different chocolate bars can you think of?

Would you like to be one of the **tasters** in a chocolate factory? Do you think you'd ever grow tired of chocolate?

chocky
crunch
gooey
chew

nutty
nougat

This group of children are going to make Chocolate Sunflower Crunch.

For this recipe you will need:

200g (8oz) plain biscuits
150g (6oz) chocolate –
    plain, or a mixture of
    plain and milk

125g (5oz) margarine
2 tbsp of water

40g (1½oz) sunflower seeds
40g (1½oz) sultanas
A little icing sugar

Dish, lightly greased with margarine

This is what you do:

1 Sandwich the biscuits between two sheets of greaseproof paper and crush them with a rolling pin.

2 Melt the margarine and chocolate with the water in a bowl. To do this place it over hot water in a saucepan. Ask for help with this.

3 Mix the melted chocolate and margarine with the biscuits, sunflower seeds and sultanas. Then pour into the greased dish.

4 When it has cooled, leave the cake to harden in the fridge for an hour or two.

5 You can decorate your cake by dusting, or sifting a little icing sugar over the top, before cutting it.

Chocolate gives you energy as it contains both **proteins** and **carbohydrates**.

It also tastes delicious!

Chocolate

My favourite flavour is chocolate
whether ice-cream or cake.
Mum always says too much of it
will give me tummy ache.

I've tried just about every chocolate bar
that shops have ever sold,
I don't think I'd swap my chocolate
if you offered me bars of gold.

When chocolate melts in my mouth
it's a really heavenly taste.
I only wish that I could buy
chocolate-flavoured toothpaste.

Glossary

Carbohydrates   The sugars and starches which are found in food and give us energy.

Cocoa butter   The rich, natural fat of the cocoa bean.

Cocoa mass   A thick liquid made by crushing the nibs of the cocoa beans.

Conche   The machine in which the liquid chocolate is stirred until it becomes smooth.

Fermentation   A chemical change in a substance brought about by heating, or through adding another ingredient.

Proteins   Substances in our food which help to build up our bodies.

Rainforests   Thick forests that grow in the hottest regions of the world.

Tasters   The tasters in a chocolate factory test some of the chocolates to make sure that they all taste nice.

Tropical   A word used to describe the very hot places in the world.

Acknowledgements
The author and publisher would like to thank The Biscuit, Cake, Chocolate and Confectionery Alliance and Mars Confectionery for their advice.

Notes for parents and teachers

Read the book with children, either individually or in groups. Talk about the illustrations as you turn each page. Ask children to name their favourite chocolate bars. In the classroom a simple chart could be produced showing favourite chocolate bars and questions written to go with it. Which is the most/least popular bar? Children could also research their families' likes and dislikes. Do older people enjoy different kinds of chocolate bars?

List the different types of chocolate that you can buy and include items that are chocolate-flavoured. Ask children to collect wrappers and make a display of these. What information is written on the wrappers? Can children design a new chocolate product and the wrapper that they would put round it? What would they call it? What ingredients would it contain? How would they advertise it? Can they think up suitable slogans? How much would it sell for? These products can be made from plasticine or clay. They could then be used for simple shopping problems.

A class letter could be written to Mars Confectionery asking for information about their product. The address is Mars Confectionery, Dundee Road, Slough SL1 4JX.

What can children find out about the areas of the world where cocoa trees grow? They could consult reference books and travel brochures. Posters could then be produced with eye-catching information and pictures showing life in tropical countries.

How would you advertise for a taster in a chocolate factory? Could children design an advertisement for a newspaper, or script something similar for a local radio broadcast? What experience would qualify someone for the post?

Talk about nutrition. Some chocolate bar wrappers give nutritional information. What other foods give us energy? Think about people who might benefit from instant energy when they need it – sportsmen and women, mountaineers, soldiers. Chocolate is often part of a survival kit.

Remind children also, that we shouldn't eat too many sweet things as they can cause tooth decay.

Children who attempt the recipe will be discovering similarities and differences in the various substances. They will discover how food changes – chocolate and margarine melt when heated, the mixture hardens when cooled. Children should also be able to talk about what they have done and to remember the order in which they prepared their Chocolate Sunflower Crunch. Simple flow charts and diagrams might be produced by older children to show the stages in the making of the recipe and in the factory production of chocolate.

The above suggestions will satisfy a number of statements of attainment in National Curriculum guidelines for English, Maths and Science at Key Stage 1.

Books to read

A Picnic of Poetry – Poems about food and drink,
   selected by Anne Harvey (Blackie 1988/Puffin 1990)
A Packet of Poems – Poems about food, selected by
   Jill Bennett (OUP, 1982)
Charlie and the Chocolate Factory by Roald Dahl
   (Puffin)
Chocolate by Jacqueline Dineen (Wayland 1990)
Chocolate, Tea and Coffee by Catherine de Sairigne
   (Moonlight, 1986)
Making Chocolates by Ruth Thomson (Franklin
   Watts, 1987)

Index